NEW HOPE STORIES

From the book of Galatians
Written 2009
Dedication

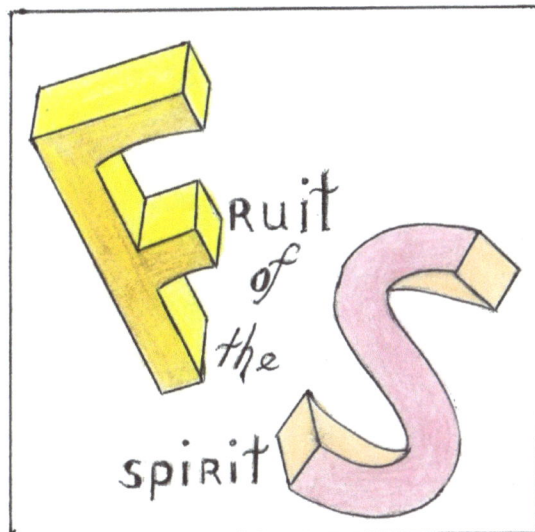

Fruit of the spirit

A short bible guide, for children of age
to be nearer to GOD and to enrich their
lives, by reflecting on their studies of the
bible, that one day they will inherit the Kingdom
of GOD.

The first fruit of the spirit, is not a banana. Do you know the answer? It's love, and it comes straight from the heart of GOD, our Lord above.

When we give our love
to each other.

It's the perfect way to be
one with GOD, and GOD
is true love.

The second fruit of the spirit, is not
an apple. It's the gift of joy, the happiness
we get, by sharing with other little
girls and boys.

When we share joy with each other
We feel like we're ten feet tall,

With a heart so big,
it could fill up a shopping mall.

The third fruit of the spirit, is not
a peach. It's something we all need,
and it's call peace.

When we rush in life, sometimes we make mistakes

and GOD, knows we can't do our best, When we hurry in haste!

The fifth fruit of the spirit, is not a grape.
It's being kind to people, we meet each
and every single day.

When you're kind to someone like a friend or your favorite pet, their friendship for you, can truly be one of life's best.

The sixth fruit of the spirit, is not
a watermelon, its being good,

obeying GOD, and our parents,
like good little children should.

When we are good girls and boys,
one day GOD, will reward us, with
lots of love and happiness
in his kingdom above.

The seventh fruit of the spirit, is not an orange, but good old faith, Knowing GOD, in His spiritual state,

Faith teaches us to believe, in things that exsist, but can't touch or see. A true example of GOD's miracle's. He teaches us to believe.

Let us pray together!

The eigthht fruit of the spirit, is not a strawberry, but our pride. It's a reminder where we come from, when we need a little charity to help us get by.

Sometimes we have to humble ourselve's and deal with life's hard Knock's, by lowering our standards, and not living like an old fancy, struting peacock!

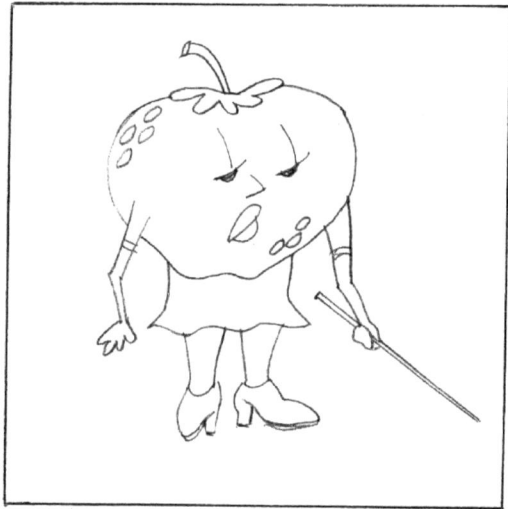

We must practice restraint, when it come's to this Rule, called self-control. Anything not good for us, is truly not good for the soul.

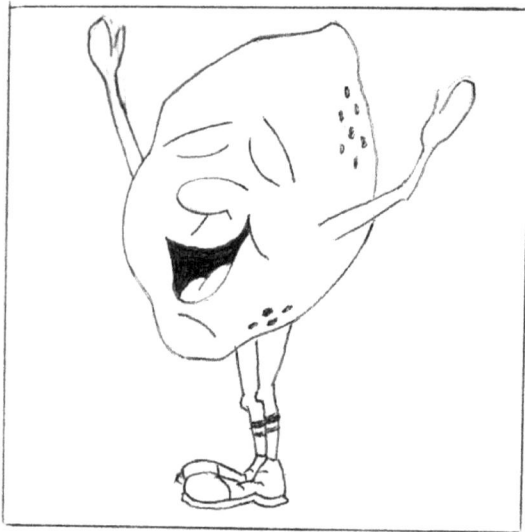

Let's meet the fruit of the spirit family.

Mr. Tate Grape

Vice Principle Mr. Tafir Pear

Sister Mary Strawberry

Gym Teacher Mr. Simmon Lemon

Shop Teacher George Orange

Written by William H. White

Pictures by W. H. White

A New Hope Story Production

PRAYER

Anna Banana

Rapple Apple

Miss Peaches Peach

Principle Bolden Watermelon

THE WORD
A Child's Guide
Grades Two to Six
Let's Pray!

Special Thanks to
Maudeva Hansford
and
Rev. Henry Harper, S.S.J.
For their inspirational insight and help.

ABOUT THE AUTHOR

4/9/53-2/28/17

William White was born in Washington D.C. He started art at Salisbury College. He sang with Skip Mahoney and the Casuals and danced on *Soul Train.* Singing and art were his passions.

www.ingramcontent.com/pod-product-compliance
Lightning Source LLC
Chambersburg PA
CBHW041556040426
42447CB00002B/197

* 9 7 8 0 9 9 9 3 3 4 2 3 2 *